Why Was Israel Called The Holy Land?

History Book for Kids
Children's Asian History

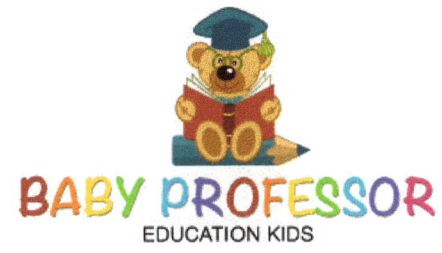

Speedy Publishing LLC
40 E. Main St. #1156
Newark, DE 19711
www.speedypublishing.com
Copyright 2017

All Rights reserved. No part of this book may be reproduced or used in any way or form or by any means whether electronic or mechanical, this means that you cannot record or photocopy any material ideas or tips that are provided in this book

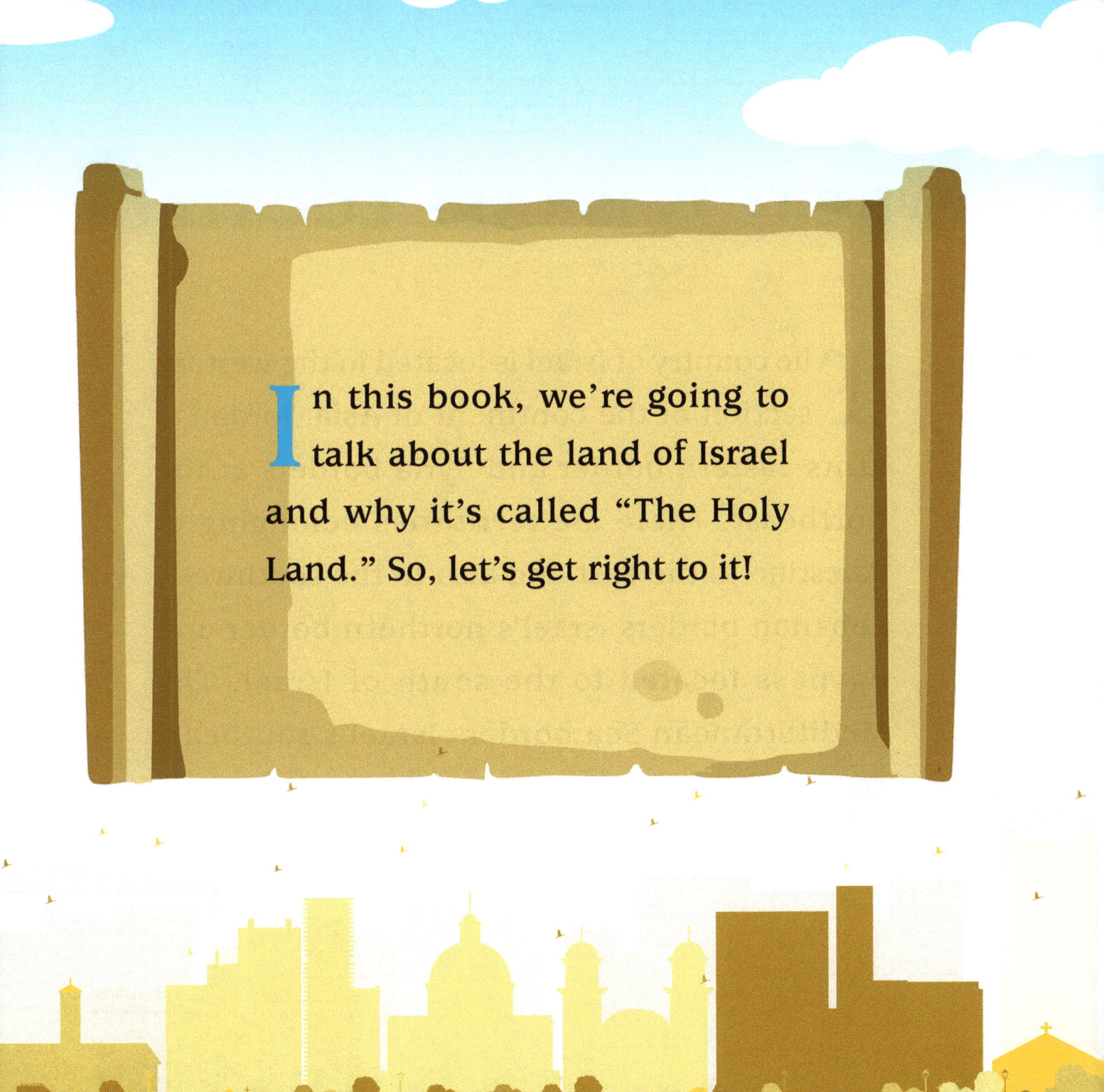

In this book, we're going to talk about the land of Israel and why it's called "The Holy Land." So, let's get right to it!

WHERE IS ISRAEL LOCATED?

The country of Israel is located in the western section of the continent of Asia. Jordan is at its eastern border and Syria borders at the northeast. There are territories belonging to Palestine to the east and also to the southwest. Lebanon borders Israel's northern border and Egypt is located to the south of Israel. The Mediterranean Sea borders Israel's southeast coast.

THAT TINY LAND IN CIRCLE IS ISRAEL

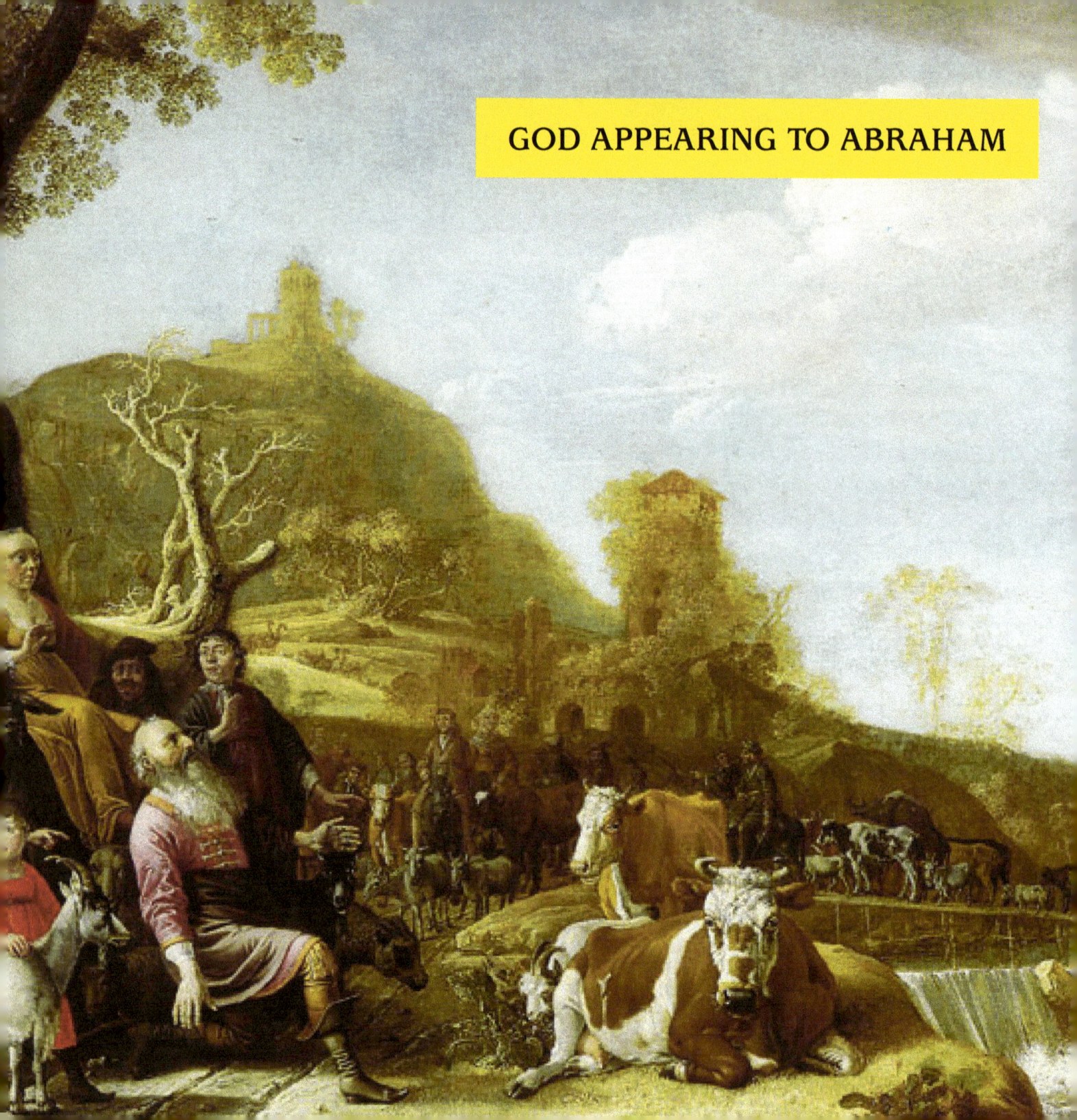
GOD APPEARING TO ABRAHAM

WHY IS ISRAEL CALLED THE HOLY LAND?

The country of Israel is often called "The Promised Land" or "The Holy Land." The reason is that in the Bible, God tells Abraham to leave his homeland. He promises Abraham that if he follows this instruction, He will give him a new land, which will be his home and the home of the generations that will come after him.

There are many places in the Bible where God repeats His promise to Abraham. God tells Abraham that his descendants will be as "numerous as the stars." This is difficult for Abraham to understand since he has no children and he's already quite old.

THE PROMISE LAND

God also tells Abraham that in the future his people will be enslaved in Egypt. At the time, the land that God promised to Abraham was called Canaan.

Eventually, everything that God told Abraham came true. Abraham became a father and over time his descendants were as numerous as the stars.

He also became a central figure in the three religions that worship one God—Judaism, Christianity, and Islam. The land that was called Canaan was renamed as "Israel" after Abraham's grandson who was called Israel. Abraham's descendants are the Jewish people.

TORAH

THE LAND OF MILK AND HONEY

The Torah is the sacred book of the Jewish people. The Torah contains the first five books of the Bible's Old Testament as well as other ancient Jewish sacred texts. In the Torah, the land of Israel is described as a wonderful land that flows with milk and with honey.

However, the land was destroyed by the many conquerors whose goal it was to make the land so barren that the Jewish people wouldn't thrive there. Since the Jewish population regained the land of Israel in 1948, there has been a huge increase in its agriculture. The land is yielding food again.

AGRICULTURE IN ISRAEL

WHY IS ISRAEL IMPORTANT TO THE JEWISH PEOPLE?

Israel is important to the Jewish people because God promised the land to them. At one point, they were slaves in Egypt and God set them free through Moses.

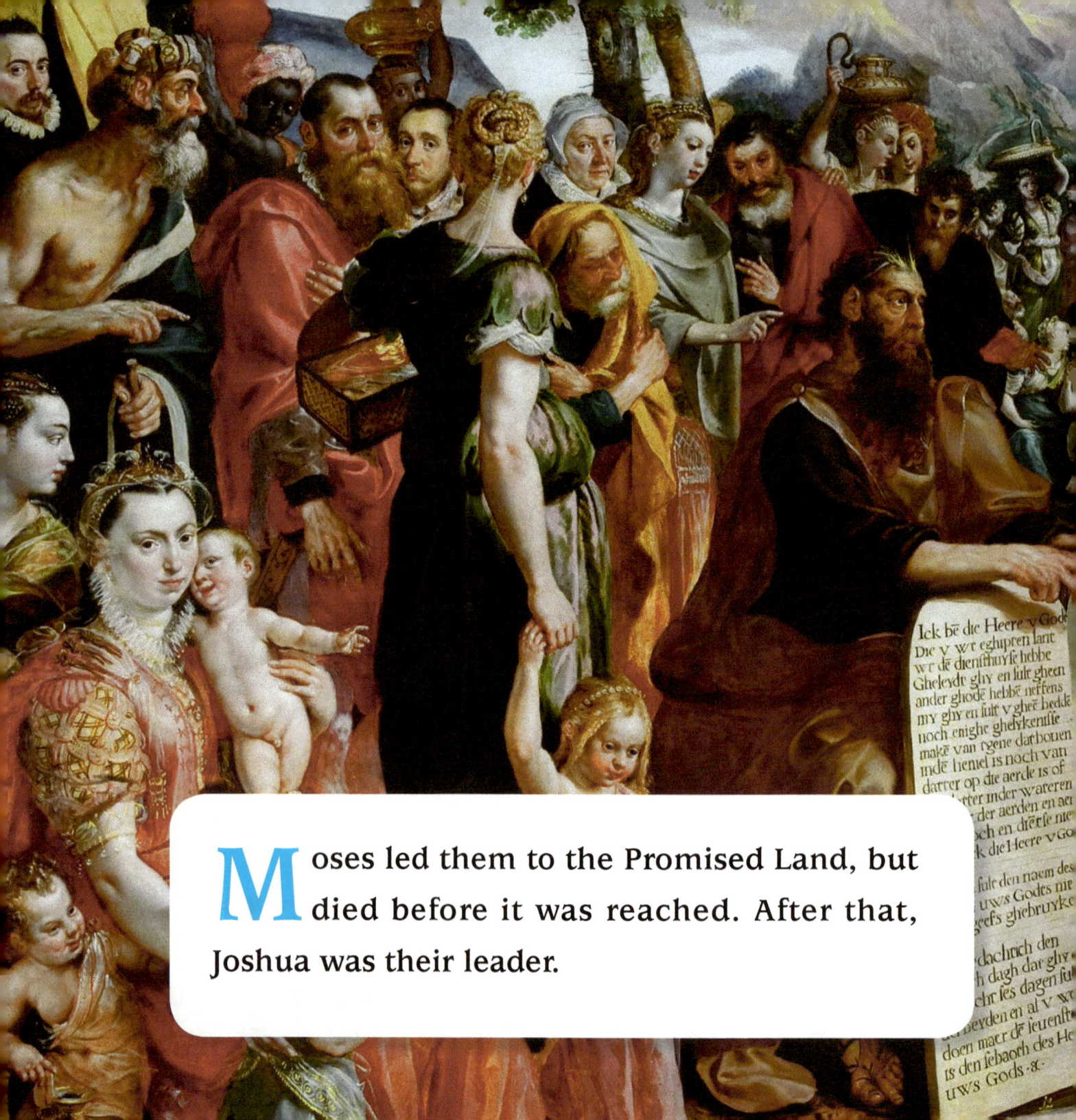

Moses led them to the Promised Land, but died before it was reached. After that, Joshua was their leader.

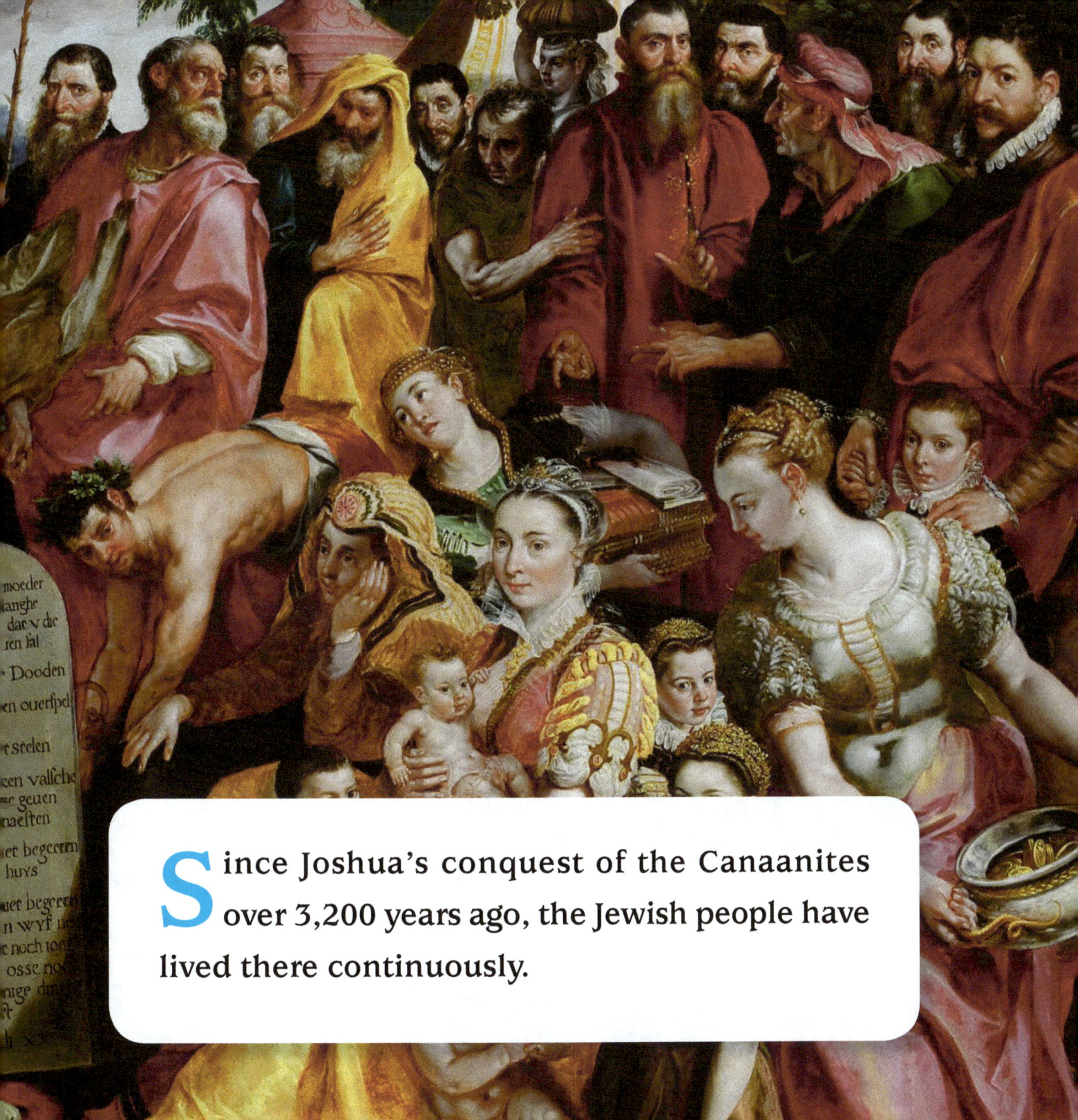

Since Joshua's conquest of the Canaanites over 3,200 years ago, the Jewish people have lived there continuously.

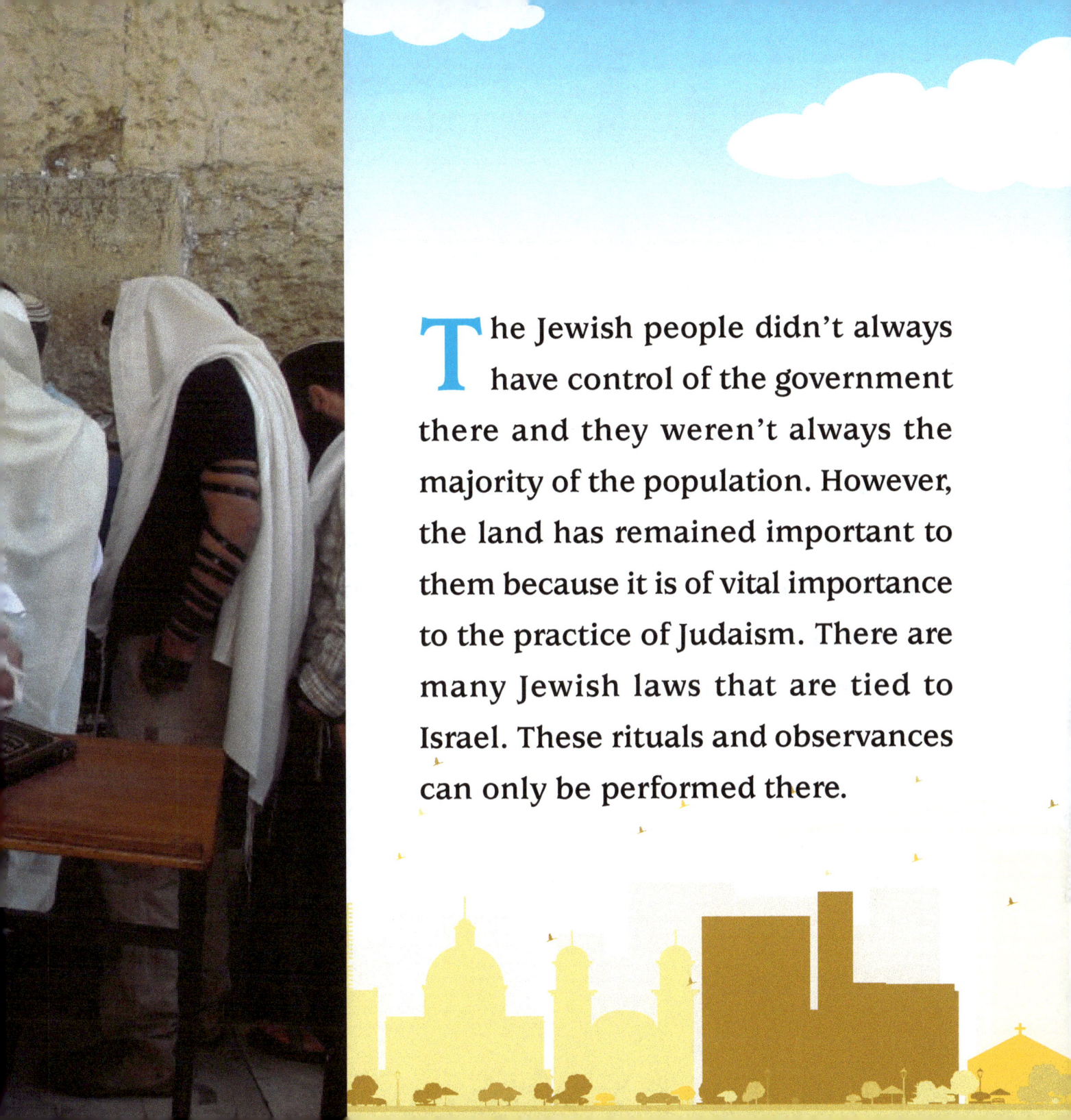

The Jewish people didn't always have control of the government there and they weren't always the majority of the population. However, the land has remained important to them because it is of vital importance to the practice of Judaism. There are many Jewish laws that are tied to Israel. These rituals and observances can only be performed there.

In fact, these laws are so important that some rabbis, who are the religious leaders of Judaism, believe it was commanded for the Jewish people to gain control of their homeland so they could live there and govern it once more.

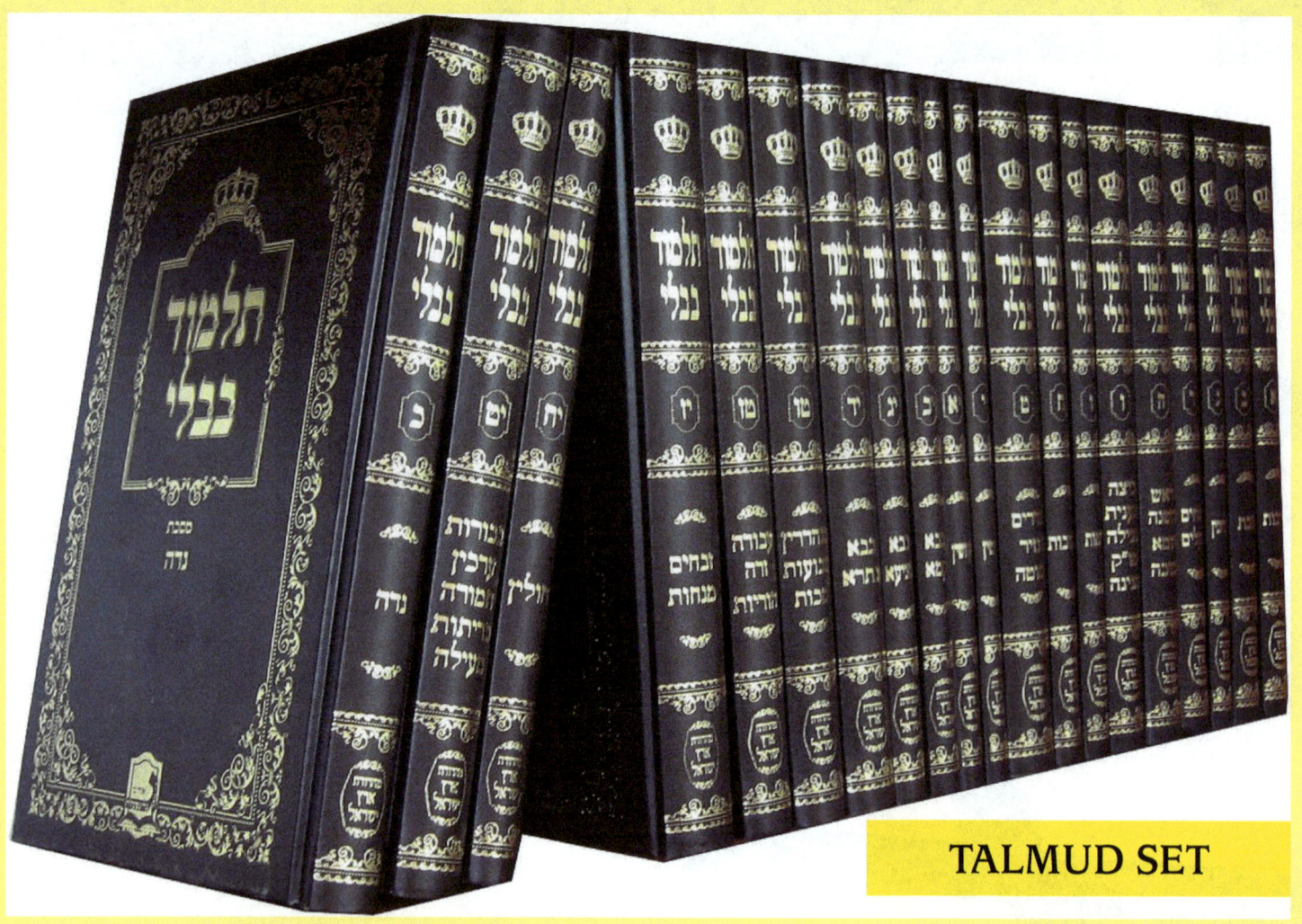

TALMUD SET

The Talmud, which is another sacred Jewish book, says that if you walk upon this Holy Land you can secure your position in the World to Come.

Throughout the history of the Jewish people they have included a return to their homeland in their daily prayers. In fact, the Jewish people believe that if they live somewhere else besides Israel that they are living "in exile."

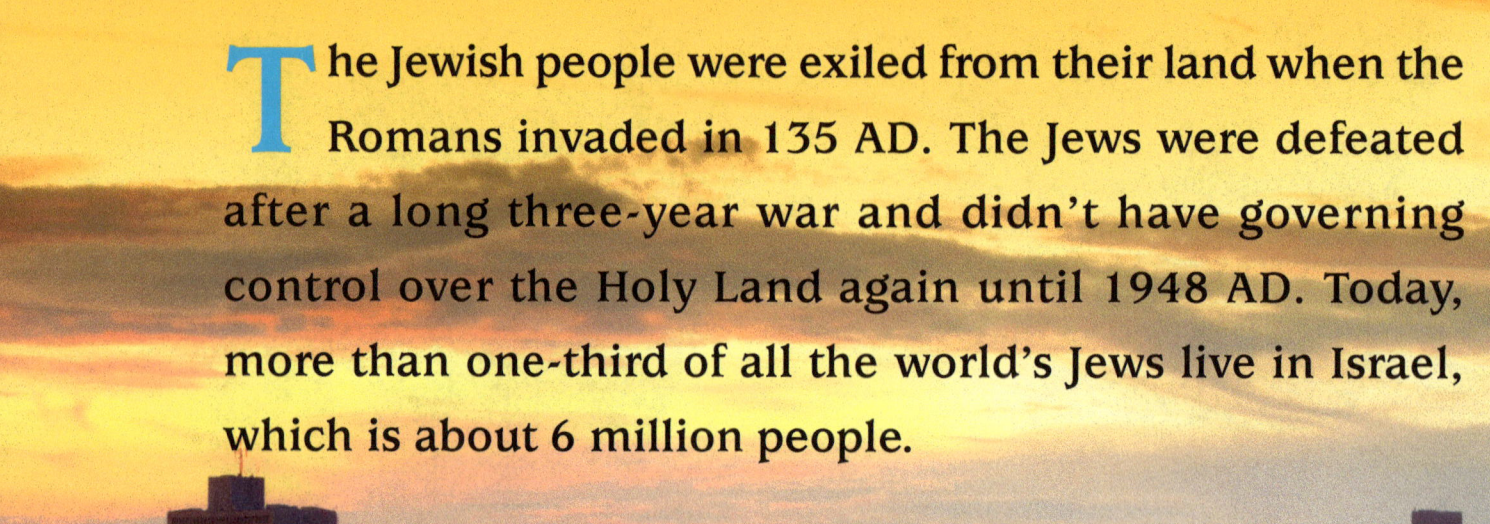

The Jewish people were exiled from their land when the Romans invaded in 135 AD. The Jews were defeated after a long three-year war and didn't have governing control over the Holy Land again until 1948 AD. Today, more than one-third of all the world's Jews live in Israel, which is about 6 million people.

THE CITY OF JERUSALEM

A BRIEF HISTORY OF ISRAEL

God gave the Promised Land to Abraham around 2000 BC and after he had sons in his old age his line of descendants began. Abraham is known as the father of the Jewish people. A thousand years later, the Kingdom of Israel was ruled by powerful and wise kings, such as King David and King Solomon.

Unfortunately, other nations wanted control over the country. In 922 BC, Israel was split into two different nations.

The northern part of the country became Israel and the southern part became Judah. Then, over the next thousand years, Israel was conquered by a series of invaders.

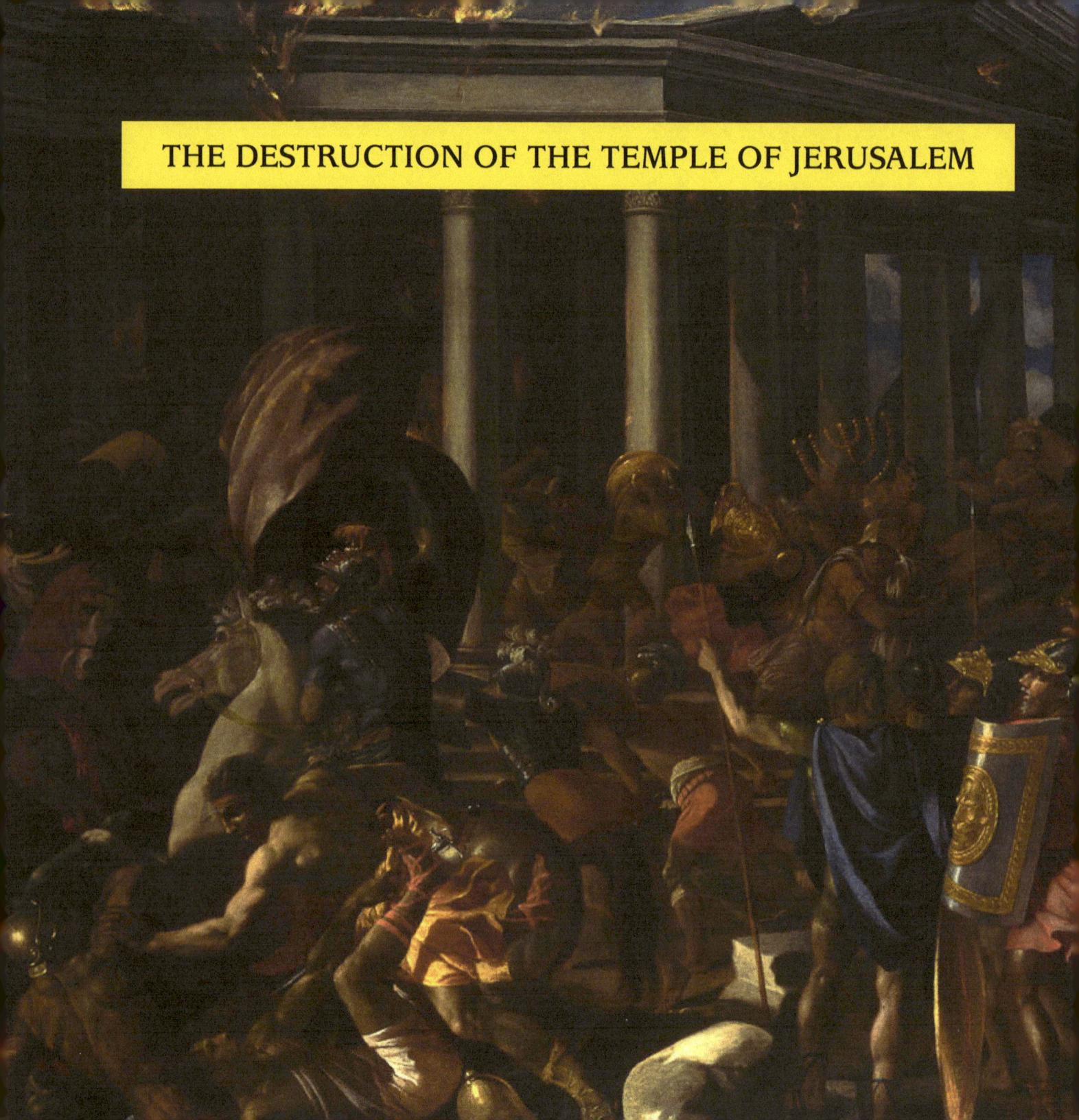

THE DESTRUCTION OF THE TEMPLE OF JERUSALEM

First, the Assyrians took control of them in 722 BC. Then, in 586 BC, the Babylonians led by Nebuchadnezzar II conquered the country of Judah, destroyed the Jewish Temple in Jerusalem, and imprisoned many of the Israelites.

In 538 BC, the King of Persia, who was called Cyrus the Great, was victorious over the Babylonians. He allowed the Jews to return to Israel. In 516 BC, the Second Temple was constructed in Jerusalem. Alexander the Great, the powerful Greek conqueror took Israel in 322 BC along with the kingdoms of Persia as well as Egypt.

THE GREAT CYRUS & KASANDAN IN THE CASTLE OF APADANA

In 167 BC, the Jewish people gained back their independence for a period of 104 years until the Romans conquered them in 37 BC. The Romans placed Herod the Great as King of Israel during that time.

Jesus Christ was born during Herod's reign and scholars believe that He was crucified around 30 AD.

Jesus was Jewish and his followers were called Christians. This is why Israel is also considered to be "The Holy Land" by Christians.

HEROD'S BANQUET

DESTRUCTION OF JERUSALEM BY THE ROMANS

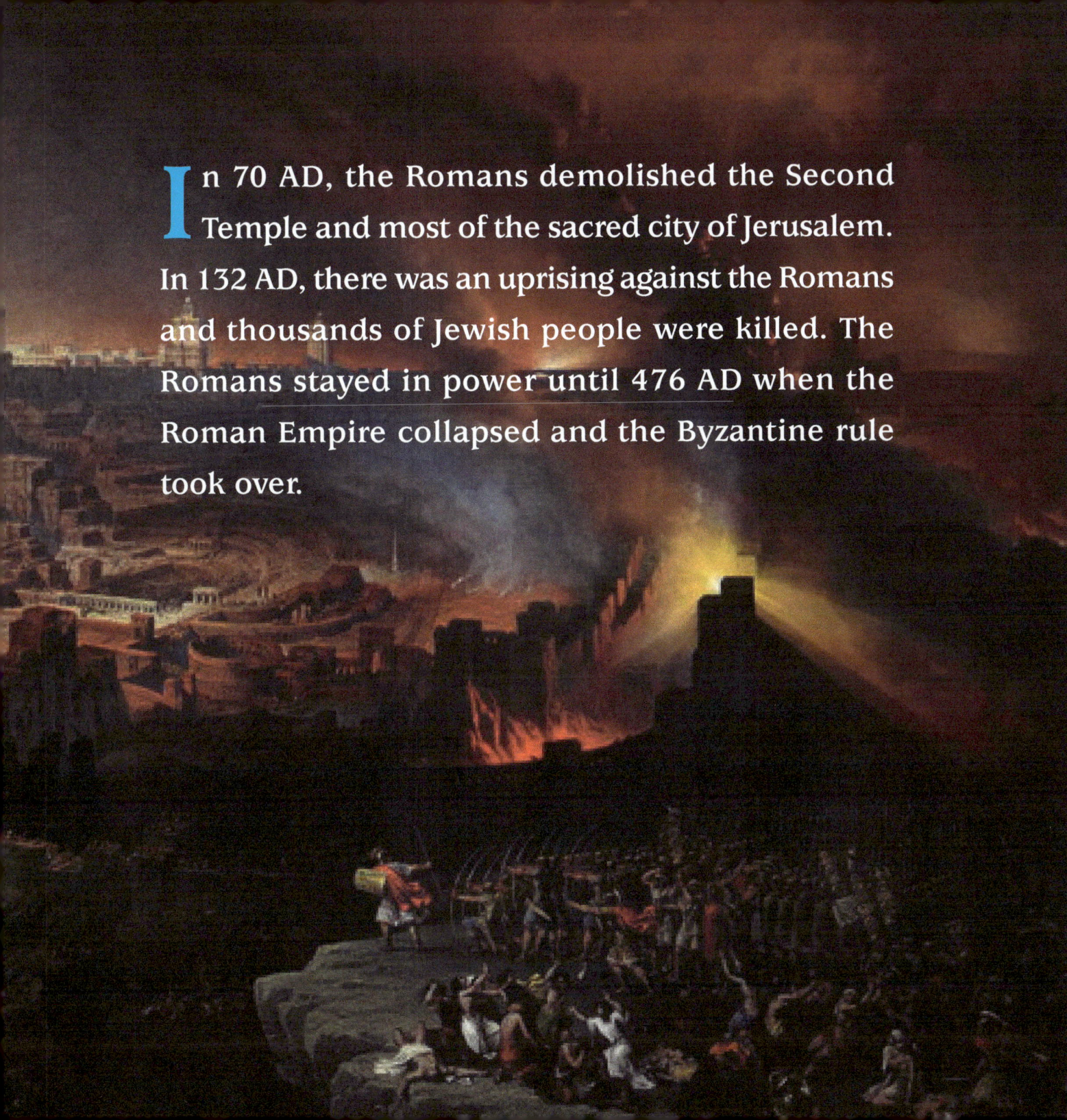

In 70 AD, the Romans demolished the Second Temple and most of the sacred city of Jerusalem. In 132 AD, there was an uprising against the Romans and thousands of Jewish people were killed. The Romans stayed in power until 476 AD when the Roman Empire collapsed and the Byzantine rule took over.

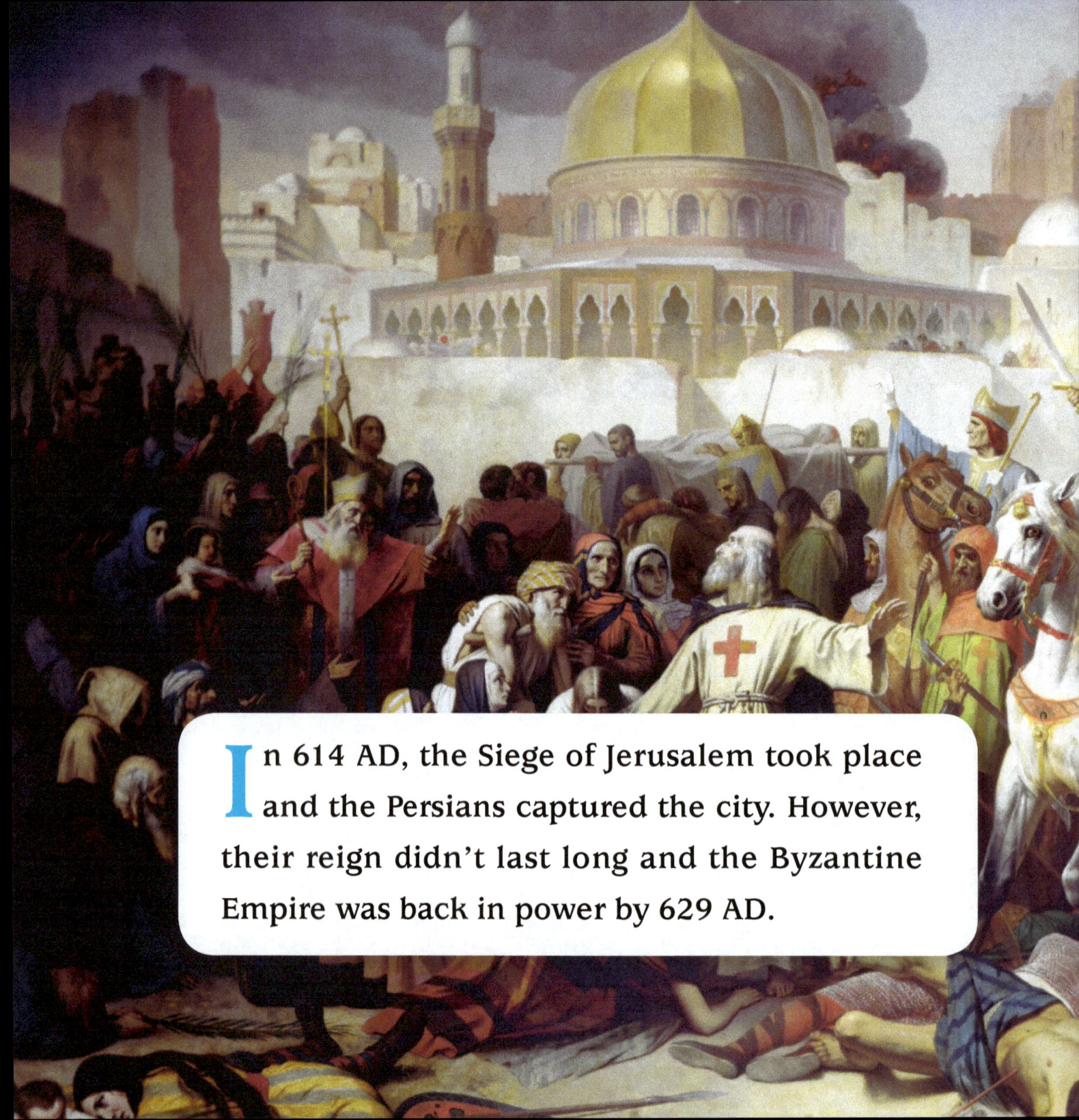

In 614 AD, the Siege of Jerusalem took place and the Persians captured the city. However, their reign didn't last long and the Byzantine Empire was back in power by 629 AD.

COUNQUEST OF JERUSALEM

In 638 AD, the Muslims overthrew Jerusalem and in 691 AD they built the Dome of the Rock Mosque on the old site of the Temple Mount. Muslims believe that Muhammad the prophet ascended into heaven from that site. This is why the region is important to the Muslims as well as to the Christians and Jews. It is considered sacred ground to three of the world's important religions.

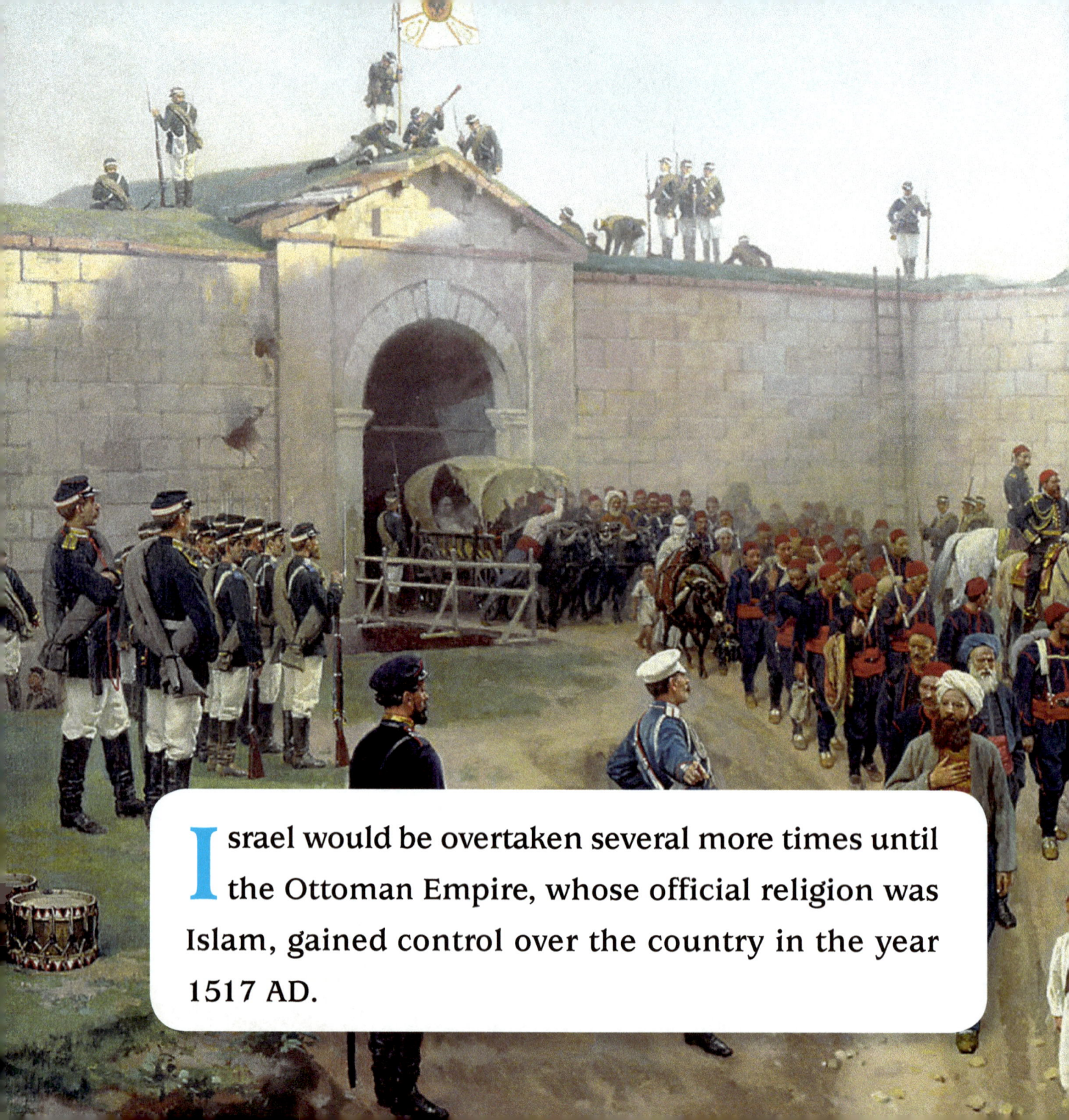

Israel would be overtaken several more times until the Ottoman Empire, whose official religion was Islam, gained control over the country in the year 1517 AD.

T he Ottoman rule lasted to the 1900s. In 1917, the Ottoman Empire was overthrown by the British and eventually this led to the pathway for the formation of an independent country of Israel.

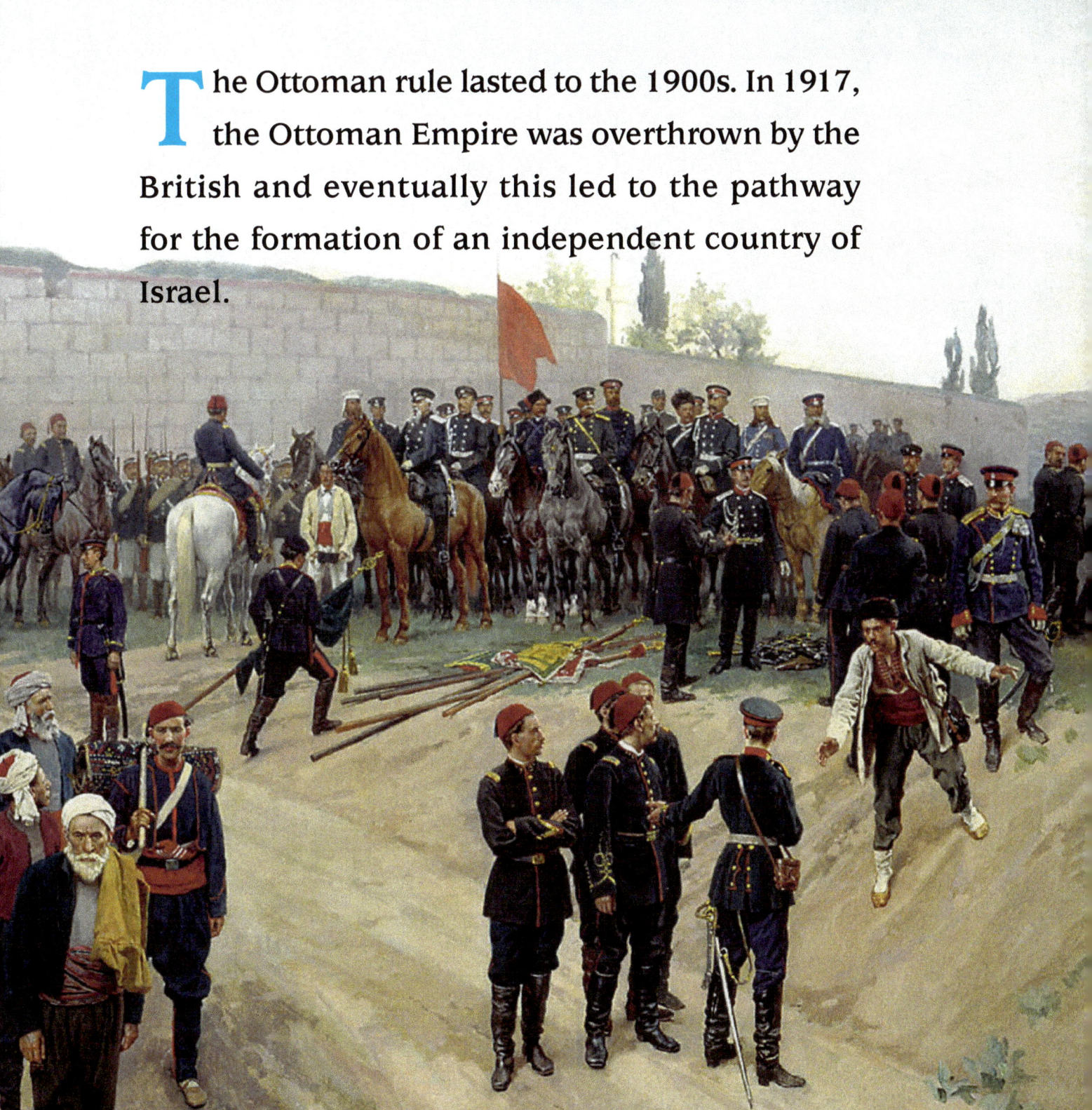

THE HOLOCAUST

During the centuries of Islamic rule, many Jewish people left to live in other areas of the world. Millions of Jews were living in Europe at the time that World War II began. Hitler despised the Jews and wanted to exterminate them. During the war, over 6 million Jewish people were killed during the Holocaust. They were sent to their deaths in concentration camps and crematoriums where they were poisoned by gas and their bodies were burned.

After World War II, the members of the United Nations voted to separate Israel between the Arabs and Jews. The Arab countries rejected their plan. On the 14th of May in 1948, the Jewish population living in the region stated that they were independent and they called their country Israel. The surrounding Arab countries began to wage war against the Jews.

DECLARATION OF STATE OF ISRAEL

The Arab-Israeli conflict started, and although a ceasefire was put into place and borders were decided, the violence continued to erupt.

There were a series of conflicts including the 1973 Yom Kippur War. Today, tensions still exist over the rights to the lands where the modern-day country of Israel is located.

SUMMARY

God promised the land of Israel to Abraham and the land is vitally important to the religion of Judaism. It's also important to Christians because Christ lived, was crucified, and ascended into heaven there. The Muslims believe that Muhammad the prophet who founded Islam ascended into heaven from the site of the Dome of the Rock in Jerusalem.

THE HOLOCAUST

The Jewish people have endured a tremendous amount of suffering throughout their history. The Germans, under the leadership of Hitler, killed over 6 million Jewish people in the Holocaust and the Arabs have been their enemies for many centuries. Today, more than one-third of the world's Jewish population live in Israel surrounded by Arab countries.

Now that you know more about the land of Israel you may want to learn more about the continent of Asia in the Baby Professor book *A Quick Look at Asia: The World's Most Populous Continent.*

Ingram Content Group UK Ltd.
Milton Keynes UK
UKHW050031290623
424178UK00007B/28